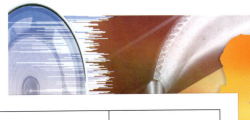

TO LISTEN

Making sense of spoken English

Lin Lougheed

Student Book 1

MACMILLAN

Macmillan Education
Between Towns Road, Oxford OX4 3PP
A division of Macmillan Publishers Limited
Companies and representatives throughout the world

ISBN-13: 978 0 333 98885 5

First published 2003

Illustrated by Kevin Hopgood, Louise Morgan, Val Saunders and
Jane Smith
Cover design by Xen Media Ltd
Cover illustration by Coneyl Jay

The publishers would like to thank Hiroshi Asano, Stuart Bowie,
James Boyd, Anthony Brewer, David Brooks, Steven R. Brownell,
Sylvia Chao, Frank Claypool, Elizabeth E. Colford, Peter Collins,
Sheelagh Conway, Ann Cunningham, Janet Denny, Joseph Dias,
Gary Farmer, Clyde Fowle, Masaki Fujimoto, William Green,
Takashi Hata, Grace Hsu, Yukari Kanzaki, Yuko Kobayashi,
Jeong Sook Lee, Mallory Leece, Pearl Lin, Peter Littlewood,
Terry McKinnon, Steve Maginn, Richard Manuel, Charlene Mills,
Harumi Nakazawa, James Pagel, Tawatchai Pattarawongvisut,
John Perkins, Harumi Nakazawa, Rube Redfield, Cristina Roberts,
Terry Roberts, Elizabeth Root, Satoshi Saito, Yoshiharu Saito,
Maria Luiza Santos, Hajime Shishido, Elliot Taback, Tadakuni
Tajiri, Andrew Todd, Kris Vicca, Genet Falconeri Watanabe,
David Wade, Robert Weschler, Sandra Wu

The authors and publishers would like to thank the following for
permission to reproduce their photographs: Alamy/H. Delespinasse
p21(a), S.Sarkis p43(4); Corbis/L.Kennedy p21(d), W.Hodges
p24(1),S.Dorantes p69(2), C.Savage p73(2); Corbis Royalty Free
Images p53; Eye Ubiquitous/A.Amsel p23(2), P.Scheult p51(1);
Getty/V.C.L p10(b), Yellow Dog Production p11(2), A.Marsland
p19(1), D.de Lossy p19(2), Color Day Production p21(b), D.Bremner
21(c), D.Bosler p24(4), A.Nagelmann p29(1), D.Harriman p29(2),
L.D.Gordon p32(2), R.McVay p32(4), C.Bissel p37(1), G.Buss p37(2),
R.Lockyer p39, T.Hopewell p41(2), F.Herholdt p46, L.Santow p51(2),
N.White p55(1), J.Gray p55(2), M.Romanelli p65(1), A.Moller p65(2),
Yellow Dog Production p69(1), S.Rowell p73(1); Robert
Harding/J.Thomas p10(d), W.Rawlings p47(2); ImageState pp 10(c),
24(2), 24(3), 27, 33(1), 41(1), 43(2), 47(1); Macmillan Archive p53;
Panos Pictures/S.Sprague p23(1), J.Holmes p32(1); Photodisc p32(3);
Powerstock pp10(a), 11(1), 33(2)

Commissioned photographs by Haddon Davies p53 (salad and pasta)

Printed and bound in Thailand

2010 2009 2008 2007

13 12 11 10 9 8

Contents

Scope and Sequence

Unit	Topic	Skills
1 First Day	Registering for class Introducing yourself Nicknames	Identifying first and family names Distinguishing between formal and informal tones
2 All About You	Data forms E-mail	Identifying personal information Distinguishing e-mail and Internet symbols
3 At the Internet Café	Break activities Internet Café Computers	Identifying actions and prices Distinguishing between amounts
4 Let's Go	Transportation	Identifying travel and transportation information Distinguishing between different pronunciations

Review 1

Unit	Topic	Skills
5 What Time Is It?	Talking about time Changing schedules Dates	Identifying time and appointments Distinguishing between dates and times
6 Describing Yourself	Describing yourself Giving physical descriptions	Identifying characteristics and habits Distinguishing between difficult pronunciations
7 How Will I Know You?	Identifying people Talking about clothes	Identifying physical descriptions and locations Distinguishing between /l/ and /r/
8 What's on TV?	Watching TV	Identifying different types of TV program Distinguishing question and statement intonation

Review 2

4

Introduction to the Student

This series will help you become more confident about the listening you do both inside and outside the classroom.

With these books you will:
- learn to listen appropriately
- learn to understand correctly
- learn to make more sense of what you hear.

You will hear a variety of sources such as conversations, messages, radio broadcasts, and other forms of real English, and you will learn to listen both for detail and for the general meaning.

As students you want to feel confident in real-life situations when you are speaking English. Through this series you will hear what real English speakers say in everyday situations, such as meeting strangers or planning a celebration, and learn to understand the words they use.

This series prepares you to react appropriately to the people you meet by helping you to make sense of the meaning behind the words they use. You will learn about the influences of a speaker's mood, location, and background on the language she or he uses.

You will gain confidence in listening and responding to everyday situations in English. You'll be able to react to the personalities of the people you meet, understand the words they use, and make sense of what you hear.

Introduction to the Teacher

This three-book listening series helps make every minute of the classroom experience as rich as the real world. The topics, the activities, the personalities, the beliefs, and the accents reflect the variety in the world around us. In the series, students meet different people, discuss different things, have different attitudes, and have different reactions.

To make the listening experience as authentic as possible, the series presents listening challenges from a variety of sources: dialogs, recorded messages, monologues, radio broadcasts, reviews, public service announcements, and weather announcements.

In these books students tackle real-world tasks that prepare them for the kind of listening they will do outside the classroom: listening for different purposes, making inferences, personalizing the experience, and making assumptions and predictions.

Students need to be actively involved in the process of learning to listen and listening to learn, because this makes learning much more effective. This is achieved by asking them to listen for a purpose, read the clues about speakers' mood, intention and background, and making students aware of the process they use in their own native language to make linguistic input comprehensible.

Students wish to react and express themselves appropriately in real-life situations. For that reason, all three books show how people react and cope in everyday situations – and they do so in a way that shows their personality, character, and attitude. By listening to, observing, and judging people in these contexts, students will learn that they too are able to express their personality when they speak English – a major step in becoming proficient in English.

1 First Day

1 What's going on?

These students are registering by last name for a class.
Check (✔) the column they should be in.

	A–H	I-R	S-Z
1. Kevin Tang	✔	✔	✔
2. Dallas Hillwood	✔		
3. Cindy White			✔
4. Mai Linh		✔	
5. Betty Sánchez			✔
6. David Crandall	✔		

2 Who's who?

Listen and check (✔) the correct name.

1. ☐ Jessica Noh
   ☐ Jessica Knowe
2. ☐ Kevin Dang
   ✔ Kevin Tang

3. ☐ Lane Morgan
   ☐ Morgan Lane
4. ☐ Carol Drexter
   ☐ Carl Dexter

3 Checking names

Listen and check (✔) who is in the class today. Then listen
again and correct the spelling of their names.

In class	Name	Correction
✓	Hiroki Aoki	Hiroko Aoki
✓	Hillwood Dallas	Dallas Hillwood
✓	Lee Toon	Toon Lee
✓	Linh Mai	Mai Linh
✓	Picot Cora	~~Cora~~ Cora Picot
✓	Sandor Silvas	Silvas Sandor.

4 Who are you?

Listen and complete the cards with people's names.

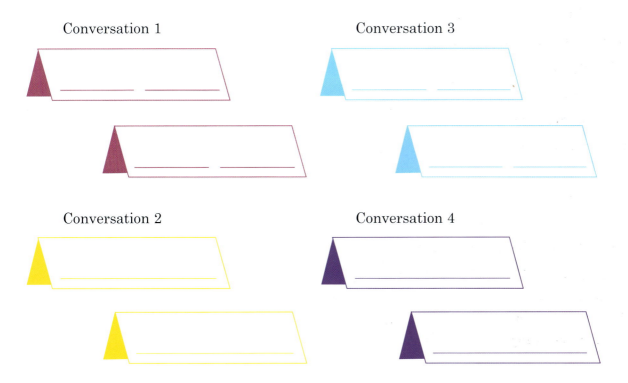

Conversation 1

Conversation 3

Conversation 2

Conversation 4

5 What's your nickname?

Listen and match the names with the correct nicknames.

Sandor	Betty
Dallas	Cindy
Cynthia	Sunny
Elizabeth	Big D

6 Train your ear

Listen to the four conversations and number the pictures.

a.

b.

c.

d.

Listen to the conversations again. Is the language formal or informal? Check (✓) the right column.

	formal	informal		formal	informal
1.	☐	☐	3.	☐	☐
2.	☐	☐	4.	☐	☐

Test yourself

Listen and circle the answer that matches the picture.

1. (A) (B) (C)   2. (A) (B) (C)

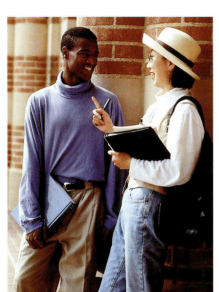   

Listen and circle the best response.

3. (A) (B) (C)   4. (A) (B) (C)

Listen to the conversation and to the question that follows. Circle the best answers.

5. (A) Mark and Lee.   6. (A) Bob.
   (B) Lee and Wong.   (B) Sleepy.
   (C) Mark and Wong.   (C) Red.

8 **Your turn**

Speak to three people and complete the chart below with their information. Use: *What's your first/last name? How do you spell it? What's your nickname?*

	Person 1	Person 2	Person 3
First name			
Last name			
Nickname			

2 All About You

Full Name

	(1) FIRST NAME		(2) LAST NAME
Mr.	Mark	P.	Grand

_____ (3) 3498 West Canton Drive
City Detroit
State/Province | Zip Code MI 48201
_____ (4) USA
_____ (5) m_grand@msu.edu
Telephone 313-554-7645
_____ (6) Teacher

1 What's going on?

The teacher is writing personal information on the board.
Complete the form with the words in the box.

E-mail Address	Country	Middle Initial
Title	Address	Occupation

2 Who's the teacher talking to?

Listen and circle the correct title. Then listen again and
check (✔) what is discussed.

Title	Last Name	First Name	Occupation	E-mail Address	Address	Zip Code
1. Mr./Mrs.	Brown					
2. Ms./Mr.	Dart					
3. Mr./Ms.	Lima					
4. Mrs./Mr.	Fernandes					
5. Ms./Mr.	King					

3 Where do you live?

Listen and correct the written information. See the example.

1.
Name: John Spencer
Address: 7405 Mason Lane

9406 Mason Lane

2.
Name: Peter Tran
Address: 1731 Riverside Drive

_____

3.
Name: Harry Rippon
Address: 500W Alton Road

_____

4.
Name: Joseph Fernandes
Address: 46 Green St.

_____

5.
Name: Kim Phan
Address: 17 First Street

_____

4 Where are you from?

Listen and put *B* next to the country where people were born
and *V* next to the country they are visiting.
Then listen again and write how long they have visited for.
See the example.

1. Van Lee
   Turkey _____
   England   V   1 week
   Vietnam   B   _____

2. Fen Wu
   United States _____
   China _____
   Japan _____

3. Marc Tirard
   Italy _____
   Korea _____
   France _____

4. Joseph Peres
   Argentina _____
   Brazil _____
   Japan _____

5. Roberto Carrera
   Mexico _____
   Hong Kong _____
   Spain _____

5 Train your ear

Even symbols have sounds. These are some common symbols found in e-mail and on the Internet.

@ means *at*   − means *hyphen*

_ means *underscore*   / means *forward slash*

• means *dot*   : means *colon*

Listen to the e-mail and Internet addresses. Write the symbols you hear. See the example.

1. **@ •**   4. _____

2. _____   5. _____

3. _____   6. _____

6 E-mail or telephone?

Listen and check (✔) how people like to be contacted. Then listen again and correct the wrong information.

1.

Alfred Lima

☐ E-mail: lima@yupi.net.bz

☐ Telephone: (55 071) 345-3340

3.

Joseph Wu

☐ E-mail: wenj@earthsat.net.tw

☐ Telephone: (886 02) 369-7556

2.

Dallas Hillwood

☐ E-mail: dallas-hillwood@naa.com

☐ Telephone: (1 714) 330-4893

4.

•••••• *Nguyen Duc* ••••••

☐ E-mail: nguyen-duc@hxm.fpt.vn

☐ Telephone: (84 04) 657-3321

7 Test yourself

Listen and circle the answer that matches the picture.

1. (A) (B) (C)   2. (A) (B) (C)

Listen and circle the best response.

3. (A) (B) (C)   4. (A) (B) (C)

**Listen to the conversation and to the question that follows.
Circle the best answer.**

5. (A) Her title.   6. (A) Reading e-mails.
   (B) Her husband's name.   (B) Writing letters.
   (C) Her correct address.   (C) Talking on the phone.

8 Your turn

Complete your own personal information form.

Full Name: _____

TITLE   FIRST NAME   MIDDLE INITIAL   LAST NAME

_____   _____   _____   _____

Address: _____

City: _____

State/Province | Zip Code: _____

Country: _____

E-mail Address: _____

Telephone: _____

Full Name: _____

TITLE   FIRST NAME   MIDDLE INITIAL   LAST NAME

_____   _____   _____   _____

Address: _____

City: _____

State/Province | Zip Code: _____

Country: _____

E-mail Address: _____

Telephone: _____

**Ask your partner for information from her/his form.
Use:** *What's your ...? What's your phone number?*

3 At the Internet Café

1 What's going on?

Look at the picture and complete the sentences. Use: *talking, waiting, checking, ordering, reading.*

1. Two people are _____ their e-mail.
2. One man at a table is _____ the newspaper.
3. A customer is _____ coffee.
4. Several people are _____ in line.
5. One woman at a table is _____ to her friends.

2 How much?

Listen and circle the price you hear.

1. Two bottles of water cost $2 / $4.
2. With $3 / $4, you can buy water and a cup of coffee.
3. A sandwich and a cup of coffee cost $6 / $7.
4. I only have $1 / $2. I'll have a cup of tea.
5. I'll have coffee, a sandwich and a piece of cake. That's $9 / $10.
6. We'll have two pieces of pie and two cups of tea. Here's $8 / $10.

3 Train your ear

Numbers *13 – 19* have a different stress from numbers 30, 40, 50, etc.
Listen to the examples:

• •
thirteen   The stress is on the second syllable.

• •
thirty   The stress is on the first syllable.

Listen and circle the numbers you hear.

1. a. 100 / 120 million gallons
   b. 16 / 60 million gallons
   c. 19 / 90 million gallons

2. a. 150 / 115 cups
   b. 40 / 14 cups
   c. 13 / 30 bottles

4 Who's taking a break?

**Listen and number the pictures. Then listen again and circle
the correct number of minutes.**

a.

10   15   20   30   minutes

c.

10   15   20   30   minutes

b.

10   15   20   30   minutes

d.

10   15   20   30   minutes

5 How much?

Listen and write the missing numbers.

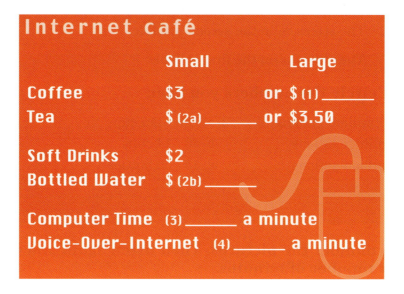

Internet café

	Small	Large
Coffee	$3	or $ (1) _____
Tea	$ (2a) _____	or $3.50
Soft Drinks	$2	
Bottled Water	$ (2b) _____	
Computer Time	(3) _____ a minute	
Voice-Over-Internet	(4) _____ a minute	

6 Pay up

Listen and number the receipts. Then listen again and complete the missing numbers.

a. Receipt ____

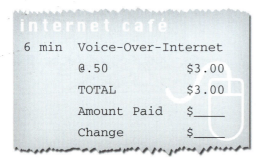

```
internet café
 6 min  Voice-Over-Internet
         @.50          $3.00
         TOTAL         $3.00
         Amount Paid   $_____
         Change        $_____
```

c. Receipt ____

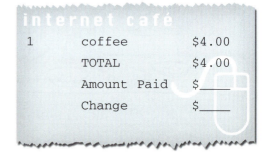

```
internet café
 1       coffee        $4.00
         TOTAL         $4.00
         Amount Paid   $_____
         Change        $_____
```

b. Receipt ____

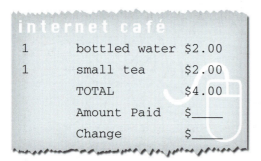

```
internet café
 1       bottled water $2.00
 1       small tea     $2.00
         TOTAL         $4.00
         Amount Paid   $_____
         Change        $_____
```

d. Receipt ____

```
internet café
 10 min Computer time
         @.30          $3.00
         TOTAL         $3.00
         Amount Paid   $_____
         Change        $_____
```

7 Test yourself

Listen and circle the answer that matches the picture.

1. (A) (B) (C)   2. (A) (B) (C)

Listen and circle the best response.

3. (A) (B) (C)   4. (A) (B) (C)

Listen to the conversation and to the question that follows. Circle the best answer.

5. (A) Pay more than $5.   6. (A) Coffee and bottled water.
   (B) Check his e-mail.   (B) Coffee and a soft drink.
   (C) Buy a computer.   (C) Just coffee.

8 Your turn

Complete the chart, then ask two people for their information. Use: *Do you use e-mail? Do you check it at work or at home? What's your e-mail address?*

E-mail	Your answer	Person 1	Person 2
Use			
Check			
Address			

4 Let's Go

1 What's going on?

Write these words in the correct categories.

car   airport   drive   plane   passenger   get on   train station   taxi
rider   on foot   get off   boat   get in   visitor   train   bus   get out
bike   fly   take   motorbike   park   tourist

People	Transportation	Action	Location

2 How are you going?

Listen and number the boxes.

a. ☐ bus   d. ☐ on foot
b. ☐ bike   e. ☐ taxi
c. ☐ car   f. ☐ train

3 What are you talking about?

Listen and number the pictures.

a.

c.

b.

d.

4 Are you going by train?

Listen and circle the correct phrase.

1. on foot / by bus
2. by car / by bus
3. by bike / by car

4. by train / by plane
5. by boat / by bicycle
6. by train / by bicycle

5 Train your ear

Sometimes it is hard to hear the difference between *on* and *off*, or *in* and *out*. Listen to the example:

She's getting off the bus. She's getting on the bus.

Listen and circle the correct word.

1. They're getting on / off the plane.
2. She's getting on / off the train.
3. He's getting on / off the plane.
4. She's getting on / off the bus.

5. He's getting on / off the bus.
6. He's getting in / out of the car.
7. They're getting on / off the train.
8. He's getting in / out of the car.

6 Now where?

Listen and number the pictures. Then listen again and write the numbers for *Track, Exit, Bus No.* and *Gate.*

a.

c.

b.

d.

7 Test yourself

Listen and circle the answer that matches the picture.

1. (A) (B) (C)   2. (A) (B) (C)

Listen and circle the best response.

3. (A) (B) (C)   4. (A) (B) (C)

Listen to the conversation and to the question that follows. Circle the best answer.

5. (A) M-14.   6. (A) Riding a bike.
   (B) M-40.   (B) Taking a walk.
   (C) N-40.   (C) Riding in a car.

8 Your turn

Complete the chart, then ask three people for their information. Use: *How are you going ...?*

	Your answer	Person 1	Person 2	Person 3
...to class?				
...home?				
...to shop?				
...on vacation?				

Review 1

1 Check over your ID

Listen and correct these ID cards.

1.

Full Name
TITLE FIRST   MIDDLE INITIAL   LAST
Mr. Eddie   Hsiao
Address
2nd Floor, No.6, Lane 42
Shuang Chen St.
City
Taipei
State/Province | Zip Code   116
Country   Taiwan
E-mail Address   HYL@carnes.org.tp
Telephone   2-596-2134
Occupation   Lawyer

2.

Full Name
TITLE FIRST
                    MIDDLE INITIAL   LAST
Ms Pamela T.   Damen
Address
Witte de Withstraat 45
City
Rotterdam
State/Province | Zip Code
Country   3012 BR
E-mail Address   Netherlands
Telephone   pam.damen@nyp.nl
Occupation   020-411-01-24
                           Artist

3.

Full Name
TITLE   FIRST   MIDDLE INITIAL   LAST
Dr.   Bruno Roberto Alvarino
Address
Avenida Presidente, 430
City
Rio de Janeiro
State/Province | Zip Code
Country   0103107.000
E-mail Address   Brazil
Telephone   balvarino_dialdin.net.br
Occupation   239-6867
                           Student

4.

Full Name
TITLE   FIRST   MIDDLE INITIAL   LAST
Mr.   Maria S.   Clarke
Address
1405 208th St. SW
City
Washington
State/Province | Zip Code   DC 20027-1432
Country   USA
E-mail Address   maria_clarke@errals.com
Telephone   202-555-2323
Occupation   Office Manager

24

Listen and circle the answer that matches the picture.

1. (A) (B) (C)

3. (A) (B) (C)

2. (A) (B) (C)

4. (A) (B) (C)

Listen and circle the best response.

5. (A) (B) (C)

6. (A) (B) (C)

7. (A) (B) (C)

8. (A) (B) (C)

Listen to the conversation and to the question that follows. Circle the best answer.

9. (A) Buying a computer.

    (B) Going to school.

    (C) Checking their e-mail.

10. (A) 6:42

    (B) 4:42

    (C) 2:42

5 What Time Is It?

1 What's going on?

Look at the picture and complete the sentences below. Use:
watch, clock, calendar, day, date, month, year, time.

1. The _____ on the wall says it's 10:15.
2. The woman in blue is pointing to her _____.
3. A man is writing the _____ November 23, 2003 on the board.
4. Two women are looking at the _____ on the wall.
5. The _____, _____, and _____ is written November 23, 2003.
6. In this picture, the _____ is 10:15.

2 What do you see?

Listen to the statements about the picture above. Circle the correct answer.

1. yes / no   4. yes / no
2. yes / no   5. yes / no
3. yes / no   6. yes / no

3 Train your ear

Dates and times in the same sentence can be confusing. Listen to the example:

The plane leaves March 7th at 7 p.m.

Listen and complete the sentences.

1. I'll see you at _____ on March _____ .
2. How about _____ of _____ , around _____ ?
3. OK. October _____ at _____ . See you then.
4. Did you say _____ on _____ _____ ?
5. See you on the _____ at _____ .
6. Right. That's tea at _____ on the _____ .

4 What time is it?

Listen and circle the correct time.

1. 2:02	10:02		4. 5:15	4:45
2. 11:45	12:15		5. 2:30	4:00
3. 3:38	3:35		6. 5:55	6:00

5 What's on your schedule?

Listen and complete the diary with these appointments: *Meet Max, Call Sue, Tennis lesson, Lunch for six, Meet Kevin at airport (Flight TA 1048).*

	Monday, 10th	Tuesday, 11th	Wednesday, 12th	Thursday, 13th	Friday, 14th
9:00	Dr.'s appointment		~~Meet Bob~~		
10:00					
11:00					
12:00	Lunch with Barry			Lunch with Mary	
1:00					
2:00				~~Computer class~~	
3:00		Get haircut			
4:00					
5:00					Shop for food
6:00				Gallery opening	
7:00					

6 Do you know when?

Listen and number the pictures. Then listen again and write the date below each picture.

a.    b.    c.    d.

_____   _____   _____   _____

7 Test yourself

Listen and circle the answer that matches the picture.

1. (A) (B) (C)   2. (A) (B) (C)

Listen and circle the best response.

3. (A) (B) (C)   4. (A) (B) (C)

Listen to the conversation and to the question that follows. Circle the best answer.

5. (A) 1984   6. (A) Wednesday, the 13th.
   (B) 1985   (B) Friday, the 13th.
   (C) 1986   (C) Thursday, the 14th

8 Your turn

Write an appointment for each day in the diary below. Then arrange appointments with other people. Use: *Which day can you ...? At what time can you ...?*

	Morning	Afternoon	Evening
Monday			
Tuesday			
Wednesday			
Thursday			
Friday			

6 Describing Yourself

1 What's going on?

Write these words in the blanks below: *hair, tall, height, brown, serious, parties, sports.*

To:	Martha
From:	Tom

My name is Tom. I'm not tall. I'm not short. I'm medium _____ .
I have brown hair and _____ eyes. I like music, movies and all _____, especially basketball.
I like _____. I'm a party animal.

To:	Tom
From:	Martha

Hi, Tom. My name is Martha. I'm _____ , but not like a basketball player. My _____ is black, but the color of my eyes is gray. I never go to the movies. I never watch sports. I never go to _____.
I am a very _____ person.

2 True or false?

Listen to the descriptions. Are the statements true or false?
Check (✓) the right box.

	Martha						*Tom*				
	1	2	3	4	5		1	2	3	4	5
True	☐	☐	☐	☐	☐		☐	☐	☐	☐	☐
False	☐	☐	☐	☐	☐		☐	☐	☐	☐	☐

3 How tall are you?

Listen and match the speakers with their heights.

speaker 1	149 cm	speaker 4
	162 cm	
speaker 2	168 cm	speaker 5
	172 cm	
speaker 3	184 cm	speaker 6
	157 cm	

4 What color is your hair today?

Listen to people talk about their old (O) and new (N) hairstyles. Write *O* or *N* beside each hairstyle picture.

1.

___

4.

___

2.

___

5.

___

3.

___

6.

___

5 What color are your eyes?

Listen to people talk about themselves and circle the incorrect information. Then listen again and correct the information.

1.

Name	Young Kun Joo
Sex	M
DOB	12/08/84
Height	187
Weight	86 kilos
Hair Color	Brown
Eye Color	Blue
Glasses	No

3.

Name	Jane Hughes
Sex	F
DOB	01/23/65
Height	157
Weight	70 kilos
Hair Color	Red
Eye Color	Blue
Glasses	No

2.

Name	Taichi Otoshi
Sex	M
DOB	04/05/77
Height	175
Weight	77 kilos
Hair Color	Black
Eye Color	Brown
Glasses	Yes

4.

Name	Carl Rossi
Sex	M
DOB	08/18/80
Height	169
Weight	73 kilos
Hair Color	White
Eye Color	Blue
Glasses	No

6 Train your ear

Sometimes some words are more difficult to identify than others. Listen and check (✓) the correct word.

1. ☐ led   ☐ red
2. ☐ don't know   ☐ know
3. ☐ tall   ☐ ball
4. ☐ life   ☐ drive
5. ☐ 1976   ☐ 1966
6. ☐ 30   ☐ 13

7 Test yourself

Listen and circle the answer that matches the picture.

1. (A) (B) (C)   2. (A) (B) (C)

Listen and circle the best response.

3. (A) (B) (C)   4. (A) (B) (C)

Listen to the conversation and to the question that follows. Circle the best answer.

5. (A) As tall as the woman.   6. (A) Red.
   (B) As tall as her brother.   (B) Black.
   (C) Taller than she is.   (C) Blond.

8 Your turn

Complete your driver's license application. Then ask your partner for her/his details and complete another application. Use: *What's your ...? Do you wear ...?*

You

🚗 APPLICATION FORM	
Name	
Sex	
DOB	
Height	
Weight	
Hair Color	
Eye Color	
Glasses	

Your partner

🚗 APPLICATION FORM	
Name	
Sex	
DOB	
Height	
Weight	
Hair Color	
Eye Color	
Glasses	

1 What's going on?

Look at the picture and complete the blanks with the correct color.

1. A man in a _____ shirt is by the information monitors.
2. A woman in a _____ dress is next to the fountain.
3. A woman in a _____ blouse is in front of the newsstand.
4. A man with a _____ briefcase is standing by the ATM.
5. A man in a _____ suit is by the main door.
6. A woman with _____ glasses is close to the taxis.

2 What color did you say?

Listen and write the number of the statement next to the color.

a. ☐
b. ☐
c. ☐
d. ☐
e. ☐
f. ☐

3 The green or the blue?

Listen and circle the correct color.

1. red / blue
2. black / yellow
3. white / brown
4. gray / purple
5. orange / green
6. black / blue

4 What will you be wearing?

Listen and check (✔) the correct picture. Then listen again and circle the correct location.

A restaurant   B station   C newsstand   D taxi stand

1.   A B C D   A B C D

2.   A B C D   A B C D

3.   A B C D   A B C D

4.   A B C D   A B C D

5 Who is lost?

Listen and write the correct letter below. Then listen again and write the name of the person who is looking.

1. _j_   _mother_   3. _____   _____

2. _____   _____   4. _____   _____

6 Train your ear

Can you hear the difference between /l/ and /r/?
Listen to the examples:

She's in the lobby. / His name is Robbie.

Listen and circle the word you hear.

1. red / lead   5. play / pray

2. green / gleen   6. belief / brief

3. glasses /grasses   7. sir / cell

4. ball / bar   8. lobby / Robbie

7 Test yourself

Listen and circle the answer that matches the picture.

1. (A) (B) (C) 2. (A) (B) (C)

Listen and circle the best response.

3. (A) (B) (C) 4. (A) (B) (C)

Listen to the conversation and to the question that follows. Circle the best answer.

5. (A) Black.
   (B) Gray.
   (C) Red.

6. (A) Orange.
   (B) Black.
   (C) Brown.

8 Your turn

Complete the chart about three people. Then get into groups. Take turns in guessing who the people are. Use: *She/He is ...*, *Her/His ... is/are ...*, *She/He wears ...*

	Person 1	Person 2	Person 3
Height			
Hair color			
Eye color			
Glasses			
Outfit			

8 What's on TV?

SALE
All TVs
20% off.
Saturday
and Sunday
only.

1 What's going on?

Look at the picture. Put the correct letter next to each TV show and match it with the correct description.

1. ___ news — people win prizes
2. ___ cartoons — you hear popular music
3. _a_ game show — you laugh at jokes
4. ___ sports — you learn about current events
5. ___ old movie — you follow a romance drama
6. ___ soap opera — you see movies in black and white
7. ___ music video — you watch golf, tennis, etc.
8. ___ comedy — you see animation for children

2 When's it on?

Listen and number the pictures. Then listen again and match the TV shows with the time of day they are usually watched.

☐ Sports

at night
after school
after dinner
Saturday morning
every evening
Sunday afternoon

☐ Black and white movies

☐ Cartoons

☐ Game shows

☐ NEWS

☐ Music videos

Train your ear

You can turn a statement into a question with intonation. Listen to the examples:

Statement: *You watch Bunny Time.*   Question: *You watch Bunny Time?*

Listen and put a question mark after the statement if it's a question.

1. You're not watching TV ____
2. Your favorite show is *Love is Always* ____
3. You saw Jackson's new music video ____
4. You didn't see the news ____
5. He's stupid ____

4 **What day's it on?**

Listen and circle the correct day.

1. They're going to watch old movies on Sunday / Monday evening.
2. She has to watch the news on Tuesday / Thursday night.
3. He wants to watch the soap opera on Sunday / Monday evening.
4. The soccer game is on Saturday / Friday night.

5 Don't miss it!

Listen to the TV announcements and number the pictures.

a.

c.

b.

d.

6 What's on tonight?

Listen and number each day. Then listen again and circle the shows you hear.

	Monday		Tuesday		Wednesday		Thursday	
	Channel 3	Channel 4	Channel 3	Channel 4	Channel 3	Channel 4	Channel 3	Channel 4
18:00	News	Cartoons	News	Cartoons	News	Cartoons	News	Cartoons
19:00	Love is Always (Soap opera)	Sports Night: Soccer	Love is Always (Soap opera)	Bunny Time (Cartoons)	Love is Always (Soap opera)	Medical Doctors (Drama)	Love is Always (Soap opera)	The Cat and Mouse Hour (Cartoons)
20:00	Romance in Ruins (Soap opera)	Sports Night: Soccer	George and Mary (Cartoons)	Pot of Gold (Game show)	Movie: Battle in the Skies	Sports Night: Baseball	The Answer Game (Game show)	Movie: Super Heroes in Action
21:00	Weekly News Review	Sports Night: Soccer	Police! (Drama)	Music Video Show	Movie: Battle in the Skies	Sports Night: Baseball	The Girl Next Door (Comedy)	Movie: Super Heroes in Action

7 Test yourself

Listen and circle the answer that matches the picture.

1. (A) (B) (C)   2. (A) (B) (C)

Listen and circle the best response.

3. (A) (B) (C)   4. (A) (B) (C)

Listen to the conversation and to the question that follows. Circle the best answer.

5. (A) on Tuesday at 9:00.   6. (A) Game show.
   (B) on Wednesday at 9:00.   (B) Drama.
   (C) on Thursday at 8:00.   (C) Comedy.

8 Your turn

What TV shows do you like to watch throughout the week? Write them on the chart. Find some people who watch the same shows and complete the chart. Use: *Do you watch ...?* *Which shows do you watch?*

	Shows I watch.	Who watches the same show?
Monday		
Tuesday		
Wednesday		
Thursday		
Friday		
Saturday		
Sunday		

Review 2

1 **What and when?**

Listen and number the activities in the correct order.

1. a. ☐ watch TV
   b. ☐ eat dinner
   c. ☐ do homework

2. a. ☐ take Mr. Lee for lunch
   b. ☐ meet Joan
   c. ☐ meet Mr. Lee at airport

3. a. ☐ coffee with John
   b. ☐ go to the dentist
   c. ☐ meet Max

2 **How will I recognize you?**

Listen and put the correct names under the pictures: *Doug, Wei, Tina, Linda, Katie, Craig.* **Then listen again and write how long they have been waiting.**

a.

_____

c.

_____

e.

_____

b.

_____

d.

_____

f.

_____

Listen and circle the answer that matches the picture.

1. (A) (B) (C)   3. (A) (B) (C)

2. (A) (B) (C)   4. (A) (B) (C)

Listen and circle the best response.

5. (A) (B) (C)   7. (A) (B) (C)
6. (A) (B) (C)   8. (A) (B) (C)

Listen to the conversation and to the question that follows.
Circle the best answer.

9. (A) Not often.   10. (A) Short, long black hair, no glasses, by the ATM.
   (B) Every week.   (B) Tall, short brown hair, glasses, by the door.
   (C) Every night.   (C) Tall, short black hair, glasses, by the taxis.

9 Planning Your Day

1 What's going on?

Look at the picture. Use these words to complete the sentences: *watching, walking, taking, sitting, surfing, reading.*

1. She's _____ a nap.
2. He's _____ on the sofa and _____ TV.
3. She's _____ the newspaper.
4. He's _____ the Internet.
5. She's _____ the dog.

2 What do your hear?

Listen to people in the picture talking about their day and number the statements.

a. ☐ This person never stops working.
b. ☐ This person likes to get out of the house.
c. ☐ This person likes seeing friends and talking on the phone.
d. ☐ This person likes to relax at home.

44

Train your ear

In spoken English, the important words in a sentence are stressed by the speaker. Listen to the examples:

Question: *Should I eat a big breakfast?*
Answer: *No, you should eat a good breakfast.*

Draw a dot (●) over the stressed word in the second sentence.

1. Did you say get up early or late?
   I said early.
2. Did you say exercise before breakfast or after breakfast?
   I said before breakfast.
3. Did you say eat your breakfast quickly?
   No, I said eat it slowly.
4. Should I take a nap after lunch?
   No, you should take a walk after lunch.
5. Is it OK to go to bed at three in the morning?
   No, you should go to bed early.

4 **What do they do every day?**

Listen and check (✔) the correct picture.

1. a  b  3. a  b

2. a 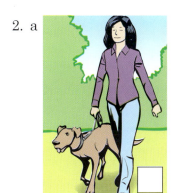 b  4. a

5 Can we meet?

Listen and match each person with the correct activity.

1. Bob   a. eat lunch
2. Mary   b. play tennis
3. Laura   c. take a nap
4. Pete   d. check e-mail

6 Stress-free

Listen and check (✔) the sentences that are correct.
Then listen again and correct the sentences that are wrong.

1. ☑ Get up early.
   ☐ Exercise ~~after~~ *before* breakfast.

2. ☐ Don't forget to eat a big breakfast.
   ☐ Eat your breakfast slowly.

3. ☐ Leave your house early.
   ☐ Get to work late.

4. ☐ Take a nap after lunch.
   ☐ Eat lunch at a restaurant or cafeteria.

5. ☐ Don't spend all evening watching TV.
   ☐ Enjoy a good lunch with your family.

6. ☐ Go to bed at two in the morning.
   ☐ Read a nice story or a magazine before you go to bed.

7 Test yourself

Listen and circle the answer that matches the picture.

1. (A) (B) (C)   2. (A) (B) (C)

Listen and circle the best response.

3. (A) (B) (C)   4. (A) (B) (C)

Listen to the conversation and to the question that follows. Circle the best answer.

5. (A) After breakfast.   6. (A) Watch TV.
   (B) Before breakfast.   (B) Read a good book.
   (C) After exercise.   (C) Surf the Internet.

8 Your turn

Ask your partner about his or her day. Use the questions on the chart. Add two questions of your own.

	Your partner
1. What time do you get up?	
2. What do you do after breakfast?	
3. Where do you eat lunch?	
4. What time do you eat dinner?	
5. What do you do in the evening?	
6.	
7.	

10 Free Time

1 What's going on?

Look at the picture and write the correct letter next to each activity below. Add two activities to the list.

1. ___ painting pictures
2. ___ collecting stamps
3. ___ reading
4. ___ playing guitar

5. ___ taking photographs
6. ___ playing computer games
7. ___ _____
8. ___ _____

2 What class are you taking?

Listen and number the classes.

a. ☐ guitar
b. ☐ photography

c. ☐ programming
d. ☐ stamp collecting

3 What are they going to do?

Listen and number the pictures.

a.

c.

b.

d.

4 Likes and dislikes

Listen and check (✔) the things Bob and Laura like to do.

	Bob		Laura
1.		going to the movies gardening	
2.		computer games fishing	
3.		playing guitar	
4.		collecting stamps	

5 Jane's list

Listen and check (✔) the four gifts that Jane will buy. Then listen again and write the correct gift for each person.

1. ☐ golf clubs   Laura

2. ☐ paint brushes   _____

3. ☐ movie tickets   Mom

4. ☐ photography books   _____

5. ☐ guitar   Mr. Wilson

6. ☐ fishing rod   _____

7. ☐ TV set   Tom

8. ☐ computer games   _____

6 Train your ear

How many syllables are in each word? Listen to the examples:

One syllable: Two syllables:
rod   *sweat|er*
stamps   *fish|ing*

Listen and check (✔) the number of syllables you hear.

	one syllable	two syllables			one syllable	two syllables
1.				5.		
2.				6.		
3.				7.		
4.				8.		

7 Test yourself

Listen and circle the answer that matches the picture.

1. (A) (B) (C)   2. (A) (B) (C)

Listen and circle the best response.

3. (A) (B) (C)   4. (A) (B) (C)

Listen to the conversation and to the question that follows. Circle the best answer.

5. (A) Send e-mail.   6. (A) It's boring.
   (B) Receive an e-mail.   (B) It's raining.
   (C) Play computer games.   (C) It's relaxing.

8 Your turn

Write three things you like to do. Ask two people what they like to do. Write them on the chart. Do you like the same things? Use: *What do you like to do? Where do you like to ...?*

Me	Person 1	Person 2
1.		
2.		
3.		

11 Let's Eat

1 What's going on?

Look at the picture and put the correct word next to each letter below. Use: *cart, eggs, apples, chicken, bananas, milk, carrots.*

a. _____
b. _____
c. _____
d. _____
e. _____
f. _____
g. _____

2 What do you see?

Listen to the statements about the picture above. Circle the correct answer.

1. yes / no
2. yes / no
3. yes / no
4. yes / no
5. yes / no
6. yes / no

3 Train your ear

Sometimes the difference between positive and negative sentences is difficult to hear. Listen to the examples:

Positive: *She's eating an apple.*   Negative: *She isn't eating an apple.*

Listen and circle the correct word.

1. He's riding / isn't riding a bike.
2. She's walking / isn't walking to the store.
3. She does / doesn't like cake.
4. This soup is / isn't good.
5. He doesn't want / does want to push the cart.
6. She would / wouldn't like a glass of milk.

4 What do they like to eat?

Listen and check (✔) the things each person likes to eat.

1.

2.

3.

4.

5 What does Bob eat?

Listen and check (✔) what Bob eats.

Breakfast	Lunch	Snack	Dinner
☐ cereal	☐ tuna sandwich	☐ donuts	☐ chicken
☐ milk	☐ chicken soup	☐ cookies	☐ salad
☐ bread	☐ salad	☐ apple	☐ rice
☐ fruit	☐ pie	☐ banana	☐ vegetables
☐ bacon	☐ cake		☐ cake
☐ eggs	☐ cookies		
☐ potatoes	☐ milk		
☐ coffee	☐ coffee		

6 Restaurant review

Listen and match each restaurant with the food it serves.

1. Joe's RESTAURANT

a.

2. Garden Café

b.

3. ART CAFÉ

c.

4. Coffeeshop

d.

Then listen again and answer the questions:

Which restaurant is best if you haven't got much time? _____

Which one is best to take your friends for lunch? _____

7 Test yourself

Listen and circle the answer that matches the picture.

1. (A) (B) (C)   2. (A) (B) (C)

Listen and circle the best response.

3. (A) (B) (C)   4. (A) (B) (C)

Listen to the conversation and to the question that follows. Circle the best answer.

5. (A) Soup.   6. (A) Cookies.
   (B) Sandwiches.   (B) Fruit.
   (C) Soup and sandwiches.   (C) Ice cream.

8 Your turn

When was the last time you went to a restaurant? What did you eat there? Write the information below. Then ask a partner and write her/his answer. Use: *The last time I went to a restaurant was ..., I ate ..., I liked/disliked ...*

12 At Home

1 What's going on?

Look at the picture and write the correct letter next to each word below.

1. ___ stove
2. ___ plant
3. ___ lamp
4. ___ sofa
5. ___ refrigerator

6. ___ picture
7. ___ sink
8. ___ chair
9. ___ table
10. ___ rug

2 What do you hear?

Listen and complete the sentences with the word you hear.

1. The_____ is on the table.
2. The _____ is under the chair.
3. The plant is on the _____ .
4. The table is in front of the _____ .
5. The _____ is next to the sink.
6. The book is under the _____ .

3 Train your ear

The words *in* and *on* sound similar. Can you hear the difference? Listen to the examples:

The book's on the table.
The table's in the living room.

Listen to the sentences and circle the word you hear.

1. in / on   6. in / on
2. in / on   7. in / on
3. in / on   8. in / on
4. in / on   9. in / on
5. in / on   10. in / on

4 A new apartment

Listen and put the words in the right place in each room.

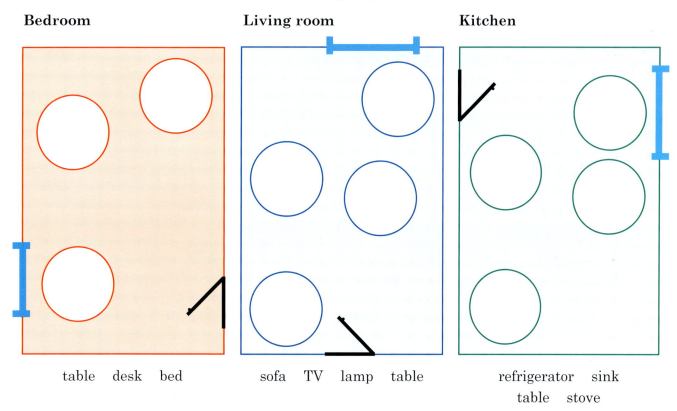

Bedroom

Living room

Kitchen

table   desk   bed

sofa   TV   lamp   table

refrigerator   sink
table   stove

5 Buying furniture

Listen and write the letter of the furniture they want to buy.

1. _____

2. _____

3. _____

4. _____

6 What's the message?

Listen and number the pictures.

a.

b.

c.

d.

7 Test yourself

Listen and circle the answer that matches the picture.

1. (A) (B) (C)   2. (A) (B) (C)

Listen and circle the best response.

3. (A) (B) (C)   4. (A) (B) (C)

Listen to the conversation and to the question that follows. Circle the best answer.

5. (A) The new table.   6. (A) On the table.
   (B) The old table.   (B) In front of the window.
   (C) The window.   (C) I got it yesterday.

8 Your turn

Listen to your partner describe her/his living room and draw it. Then change roles. Use: *next to, behind, in front of, under, across from, over, on, in.*

Your partner's living room

Review 3

1 ## Things have to change!

Listen and number the pictures of the speakers. Then listen again and circle the correct wish. **A** *I'd like a big plate of spaghetti.* **B** *Let's put my chair by the window.* **C** *I think my hobby will be photography.* **D** *I want to be in my living room.*

a.

A B C D

c.

A B C D

b.

A B C D

d.

A B C D

Listen and circle the answer that matches the picture.

1. (A) (B) (C)   3. (A) (B) (C)

2. (A) (B) (C)   4. (A) (B) (C)

Listen and circle the best response.

5. (A) (B) (C)   7. (A) (B) (C)
6. (A) (B) (C)   8. (A) (B) (C)

Listen to the conversation and the question that follows.
Circle the best answer.

9. (A) A sofa and a chair.   10. (A) Knitting and stamp collecting.
   (B) Only a rug.   (B) Cooking Chinese food and stamp collecting.
   (C) A TV in the corner.   (C) Knitting and cooking Chinese food.

13 Sunny or Cloudy?

1.

2.

3.

4.

1 What's going on?

Look at the pictures and then check (✓) the appropriate columns in the two charts.

CLOTHING	1.	2.	3.	4.
umbrella				
boots				
scarf				
raincoat				
gloves				
hat				
sunglasses				
shorts				
T-shirt				
parka				

WEATHER	1.	2.	3.	4.
windy				
cloudy				
sunny				
thunder				
wet				
lightning				
cold				
stormy				
humid				
warm				

2 What do you see?

Listen to the statements about the pictures above. Circle the correct answer.

1. yes / no   4. yes / no
2. yes / no   5. yes / no
3. yes / no   6. yes / no

3 Train your ear

The plural in English is pronounced in three ways. Listen to the examples:

/s/ = hats   /z/ = shoes   /ɪz/ = sunglasses

Listen and check (✓) the sound you hear.

	/s/	/z/	/ɪz/
1.			
2.			
3.			
4.			

	/s/	/z/	/ɪz/
5.			
6.			
7.			
8.			

4 Weekend activities

Listen and number the pictures.

a.

c.

b.

d.

5 What's the temperature?

Listen and write the missing information on the chart.

	January 19th	January 20th
High Temperature	77°F at 2:00 p.m.	50°F at 2:30 p.m.
Low Temperature	____ at 6:45 a.m.	30°F at __ a.m.
Normal High	65°F (18°C)	38°F (3°C)
Normal Low	____°F (7°C)	____°F (–2°C)
Record High	88°F in ____	65°F in 1928
Record Low	32°F in 1918	____°F in 1981

6 What will the weather be?

Listen and check (✔) the weather for each day. Then listen
again and write the high and low temperatures.

	☀	☁	⚡	❄	🌧
Monday High _____ Low _____					
Tuesday High _____ Low _____					
Wednesday High _____ Low _____					
Thursday High _____ Low _____					
Friday High _____ Low _____					

Test yourself

Listen and circle the answer that matches the picture.

1. (A) (B) (C)   2. (A) (B) (C)

Listen and circle the best response.

3. (A) (B) (C)   4. (A) (B) (C)

Listen to the conversation and to the question that follows. Circle the best answer.

5. (A) A scarf.   6. (A) It's snowing.
   (B) Gloves.   (B) It's morning.
   (C) An umbrella.   (C) It's sunny.

8 **Your turn**

Complete the chart below with local weather information. Compare your chart with that of your partner. Check your prediction next week. Use: *It will be a ...,   We will have ...*

Today's weather	Forecast for the weekend

14 On the Block

1 What's going on?

Look at the picture and write the correct letter (a–h from the picture) next to each activity or place below.

1. ____ buy the food I need
2. ____ exercise
3. ____ go see a movie
4. ____ dry clean my clothes

5. ____ mail a letter
6. ____ meet my friends for coffee
7. ____ ride my bicycle
8. ____ sit quietly

2 What do you see?

Listen to the statements about the picture above. Circle the correct answer.

1. yes / no
2. yes / no
3. yes / no

4. yes / no
5. yes / no
6. yes / no

3 How was your day?

Listen and number the activities. One activity is wrong.

a. Things to do:
- ☐ visit the post office
- ☐ go to the bank
- ☐ stop for a coffee
- ☐ go to the dry cleaners

b. Things to do:
- ☐ go to the doctor
- ☐ shop at the store
- ☐ go to the post office
- ☐ visit the dentist

c. Things to do:
- ☐ go to the mall
- ☐ do the gardening
- ☐ go shopping
- ☐ take the kids to school

d. Things to do:
- ☐ park the car
- ☐ go to the bar
- ☐ eat
- ☐ go to a movie

4 Life on my block

Listen and check (✔) the correct picture.

1.

3.

2.

4.

5 How long have you lived here?

Listen and write the number of the house.

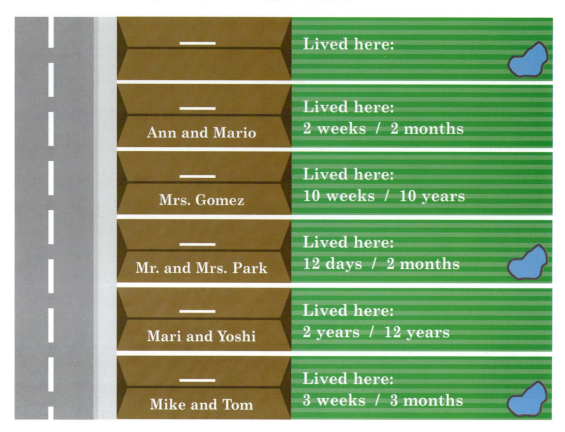

Then listen again and circle how long they have lived there.

6 Train your ear

**In spoken English unstressed words are difficult to hear.
Listen to the examples:**

The bank is next to the park.

**Listen to the sentences and underline the words which are
not stressed.**

1. Why don't you meet me in the center of town?
2. I'm going to leave the coffee shop around ten.
3. Is there a bank on this block?
4. There are some kids in the park.
5. I'm going out for lunch today.
6. I'll meet you outside the Cineplex at three, OK?

Test yourself

Listen and circle the answer that matches the picture.

1. (A) (B) (C)   2. (A) (B) (C)

Listen and circle the best response.

3. (A) (B) (C)   4. (A) (B) (C)

Listen to the conversation and to the question that follows.
Circle the best answer.

5. (A) In the lobby.   6. (A) He missed the bus.
   (B) In his office.   (B) He got a parking ticket.
   (C) In the park.   (C) He lost his ticket.

8 **Your turn**

Work with your partner and draw your ideal neighborhood.
Use: *outside, opposite, next to, the other side of.*

15 Downtown

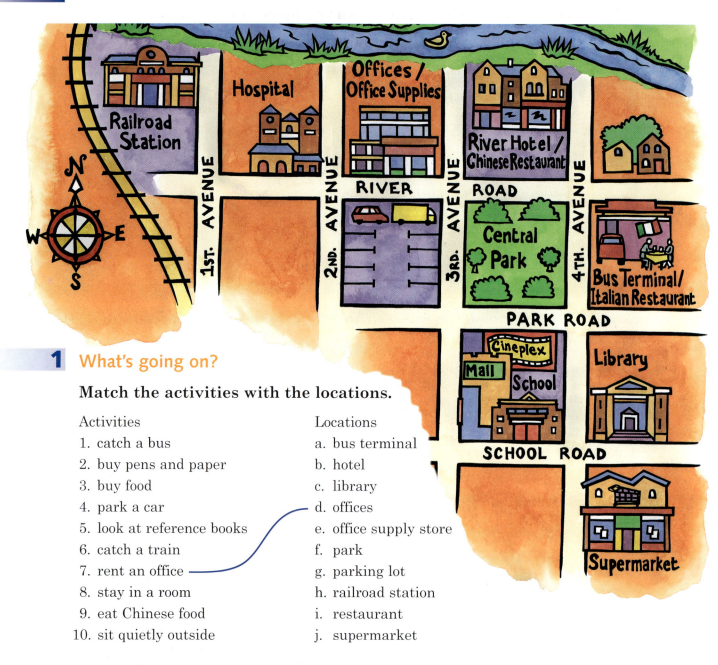

1 What's going on?

Match the activities with the locations.

Activities	Locations
1. catch a bus	a. bus terminal
2. buy pens and paper	b. hotel
3. buy food	c. library
4. park a car	d. offices
5. look at reference books	e. office supply store
6. catch a train	f. park
7. rent an office	g. parking lot
8. stay in a room	h. railroad station
9. eat Chinese food	i. restaurant
10. sit quietly outside	j. supermarket

2 What's there?

Look at the map. Listen to each description and the three places that follow it. Write the correct place.

1. Italian restaurant

2. _____

3. _____

4. _____

5. _____

6. _____

3 Can you help me?

Listen and match each speaker with the place she/he wants to go.

speaker 1   airport   speaker 3
                               hospital
                        Italian restaurant
                            supermarket
                            bus terminal
speaker 2   school   speaker 4
                               library
                                mall
                        Chinese restaurant

4 Where am I?

Where are the speakers? Look at the map on page 70. Listen and number each picture.

a.   b.   c.   d.

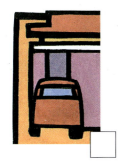         

Where do they want to go? Listen again and number each picture.

a.   b.   c.   d.

5 Come on down!

Listen and number the ads. Then listen again and check (✔) the correct items.

OFFICE SUPPLY STORE

- ☐ Book bags
- ☐ Notebooks
- ☐ Pencils
- ☐ Photocopiers
- ☐ Paper
- ☐ Pens
- ☐ Printers
- ☐ Computer supplies
- ☐ Fax machines
- ☐ Staplers
- ☐ Computer equipment

☐

★ Cineplex ★

- ☐ 10 Screens
- ☐ Child care center
- ☐ Free parking
- ☐ Free popcorn
- ☐ New café
- ☐ Old favorites
- ☐ Latest released movies

☐

Supermarket

REDUCED BY 10%

- ☐ All dairy products
- ☐ All meat
- ☐ All fruit
- ☐ All seafood
- ☐ All housewares
- ☐ All vegetables

☐

Italian Restaurant

MENU

- ☐ SPAGHETTI
- ☐ MEATBALLS
- ☐ SALAD
- ☐ CHILDREN EAT FREE
- ☐ FREE DESSERT WITH TWO ENTREES
- ☐ FREE SALAD WITH MEAL

Italian Restaurant

☐

6 Train your ear

Contractions such as *I'll* (I will) may be difficult to hear. Listen to the examples:

I go to the mall every Saturday. (present tense)
I'll go to the mall next Saturday. (future tense)

Listen to the sentences and circle the word you hear.

1. I / I'll
2. We / We'll
3. They / They'll
4. I / I'll
5. I / I'll
6. We / We'll
7. They / They'll
8. I / I'll
9. You / You'll
10. We / We'll

72

7 Test yourself

Listen and circle the answer that matches the picture.

1. (A) (B) (C)   2. (A) (B) (C)

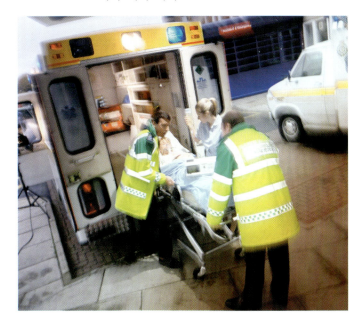 

Listen and circle the best response.

3. (A) (B) (C)   4. (A) (B) (C)

Listen to the conversation and to the question that follows. Circle the best answer.

5. (A) Exercise more.   6. (A) Have some coffee.
   (B) Eat less.   (B) Start a fitness program.
   (C) Leave him alone.   (C) Have copies made.

8 Your turn

When did you last go shopping? Complete the chart and ask two other people.

	You	Person 1	Person 2
Where did you shop?			
What did you buy there?			
How much did you spend?			

16 Let's Celebrate

1 What's going on?

Look at the list of things we do to celebrate holidays. Check (✔) the things you see in the picture.

1. ☐ have a picnic
2. ☐ go to the beach
3. ☐ go dancing
4. ☐ dress up
5. ☐ watch a parade
6. ☐ send cards
7. ☐ watch fireworks
8. ☐ put up decorations
9. ☐ give gifts
10. ☐ spend time with family
11. ☐ have a big dinner
12. ☐ visit friends

2 Talking about celebrations

Listen and circle the correct word.

1. The woman thinks birthdays are / aren't fun.
2. He wants / doesn't want to have a picnic.
3. She sent / didn't send a Mother's Day card.
4. People are / aren't happy now.

3 Train your ear

Listen to these statements and check (✔) whether the speaker sounds interested or bored. Listen to the examples:

There's a big parade today.   (interested)
There's a big parade today.   (bored)

	Interested	Bored
1.		
2.		
3.		

	Interested	Bored
4.		
5.		
6.		

4 Celebrating the holidays

Listen and number the pictures. Then listen again and match the pictures with the activities.

a.

stay at home and rest

stay up late

b.

have dinner and a cake

have a big dinner with family

c.

buy flowers

stay at home and rest

d.

go dancing

buy a card and chocolates

5 Holiday plans

Listen and check (✔) the correct picture.

1.

3.

2.

4.

6 What, where, when?

Listen and number each holiday event. Then listen again and match each holiday event with the correct place and write the correct time.

a. ☐ National Day trip
   Time: _____
b. ☐ Fireworks
   Time: _____
c. ☐ Sale
   Time: _____
d. ☐ Dance
   Time: _____

Test yourself

Listen and circle the answer that matches the picture.

1. (A) (B) (C)   2. (A) (B) (C)

Listen and circle the best response.

3. (A) (B) (C)   4. (A) (B) (C)

Listen to the conversation and to the question that follows. Circle the best answer.

5. (A) In the park.   6. (A) Cake.
   (B) I think so.   (B) Potato salad.
   (C) At 9:30.   (C) Soft drinks.

8 Your turn

Ask three people about their favorite holiday. Complete the chart below. Use: *What's your favorite holiday?*

Name	Favorite holiday	Date	How do you celebrate it?

Review 4

What's happening?

Listen and check (✔) the correct information.

Who	Event	Location	Weather
1.	☑ New Year's day ☐ National Day ☐ Mother's Day ☐ Valentine's Day	☑ Office Supply Store ☐ Office ☐ Park ☐ Computer Store	☐ Rainy ☐ Windy ☑ Cold ☐ Snowy
2.	☐ New Year's day ☑ National Day ☐ Mother's Day ☐ Valentine's Day	☐ Office Supply Store ☑ Office ☐ Park ☐ Computer Store	☐ Rainy ☐ Windy ☐ Cold ☑ Snowy
3.	☐ New Year's day ☐ National Day ☐ Mother's Day ☑ Valentine's Day	☐ Office Supply Store ☐ Office ☐ Park ☐ Computer Store	☐ Rainy ☐ Windy ☐ Cold ☐ Snowy
4.	☐ New Year's day ☐ National Day ☐ Mother's Day ☐ Valentine's Day	☐ Office Supply Store ☐ Office ☐ Park ☐ Computer Store	☐ Rainy ☐ Windy ☐ Cold ☐ Snowy

2 Conversation review

Listen and circle the answer that matches the picture.

1.

(A) (B) (C)

3.

(A) (B) (C)

2.

(A) (B) (C)

4.

(A) (B) (C)

Listen and circle the best response.

5. (A) (B) (C)

6. (A) (B) (C)

7. (A) (B) (C)

8. (A) (B) (C)

Listen to the conversation and to the question that follows. Circle the best answer.

9. (A) One building with everything in it.

(B) The problems of urban living.

(C) The bad weather.

10. (A) Summer.

(B) Spring.

(C) Winter.